To

From

A
DON'T SWEAT
THE SMALL STUFF
Treasury

Also by the Author

Don't Sweat the Small Stuff in Love
Don't Sweat the Small Stuff at Work
Don't Sweat the Small Stuff with Your Family
Don't Worry, Make Money
Don't Sweat the Small Stuff . . . And It's All Small Stuff
Slowing Down to the Speed of Life (with Joseph Bailey)
Handbook for the Heart (with Benjamin Shield)
Handbook for the Soul (with Benjamin Shield)
Shortcut Through Therapy
You Can Feel Good Again
You Can Be Happy No Matter What

Don't Sweat the Small Stuff Treasuries:

A Special Selection for Fathers
A Special Selection for Mothers
A Special Selection for Graduates
A Special Selection for Teachers
A Special Collection for Friends
A Special Collection for New Parents
A Special Collection for the Office

DON'T SWEAT THE SMALL STUFF

Treasury

A Special Collection
for Newlyweds

Richard Carlson, Ph.D.

A Don't Sweat the Small Stuff Treasury
A Special Collection for Newlyweds

Copyright © 2000, Richard Carlson, Ph.D.

ISBN: 0-7868-6623-3

Library of Congress Catalog Card Number: 99-37515

FIRST EDITION

10 9 8 7 6 5 4 3 2 1

A
DON'T SWEAT
THE SMALL STUFF
Treasury

Contents

Introduction   xiii

1. Don't Interrupt Others or Finish
   Their Sentences   1

2. Be the First One to Act Loving
   or Reach Out   4

3. Become Aware of Your Moods and
   Don't Allow Yourself to Be Fooled
   by the Low Ones   7

4. Look Beyond Behavior   11

5. Choose Being Kind over Being Right   13

6. When in Doubt about Whose Turn
   It Is to Take Out the Trash, Go Ahead
   and Take it Out   17

7. Develop Your Own Helping Rituals   20

8. Resist the Urge to Criticize   23

9. Just for Fun, Agree with Criticism Directed Toward You (Then Watch It Go Away)   26

10. Relax   29

11. Think of What You Have Instead of What You Want   32

12. Be Willing to Learn from Friends and Family   35

13. Give Up on the Idea that "More Is Better"   38

14. Keep in Mind that a Happy Spouse Is a Helping Spouse   42

15. Listen to Her (and Him Too)   47

16. Keep Your Promises   52

17. Never Miss a Chance to Say "I Love You"   57

18. Fill Your Home with Evidence of Love   61

19. Start the Day with Love, Live the Day with Love, End the Day with Love   65

20. Never, Ever, Take Your Spouse
    (or Significant Other) for Granted   68

21. Appreciate your In-Laws   74

22. Work on Absolute Acceptance of Those
    You Love Most   78

23. Don't Sweat the Little Quirks   82

24. Reverse Roles with Your Spouse   86

25. Don't Go to Bed Mad   91

Introduction

Let me begin by saying, "Congratulations!" Being a proud supporter of marriage and family, I'm delighted for you and wish you a lifetime of happiness.

It's hard to imagine that something as wonderful as being a newlywed could possibly be stressful—but, truthfully, it often is! So much has changed and so much is new. For the most part, of course, the changes are welcome. But, as is often the case with major life changes, some mental adjustments need to be made.

Ironically, I'm writing this introduction on the eve of my fourteenth wedding anniversary. Looking back, being a newlywed was a very special time. It was a time filled with hopes and dreams, and a commitment to one another to be friends and partners for life. Yet, this special time wasn't without some stress. Being so used to doing things our own ways, we had to learn to compromise, to give and take, see the bigger picture and take things in stride. We also had to learn to work together, take each other's preferences, insecurities, and goals to heart, and to take ourselves, each other, and our many quirks less seriously. Whoever you are and regardless of how much you love each other, it's likely that you too will experience at least a little frustration. Don't worry about it; it seems to go with the territory!

On the "love front," things have worked out really well for Kristine and me. We've managed to not only remain friends, but are also still very much in love as well. In fact, our love has grown in many beautiful ways. Although there are many factors that have undoubtedly contributed to the success of our marriage, there are some ideas that, I believe, stand out as being particularly important.

I have carefully selected strategies from each of my *Don't Sweat* books that, looking back, I feel contributed the most to making my life as a newlywed as joyful as possible. I now feel that, had I not utilized these particular strategies, my experience as a newlywed would have been substantially more stressful. It's my hope that as you read these selections and put them into practice, you too will dance through this very special and important time in your life with a minimal amount of stress.

I truly hope you enjoy this little book and that it serves you well. Again, I'm very happy for you and wish you great joy in your new marriage!

Treasure each other,

Richard Carlson

Don't Interrupt Others or Finish Their Sentences

It wasn't until a few years ago that I realized how often I interrupted others and/or finished their sentences. Shortly thereafter, I also realized how destructive this habit was, not only to the respect and love I received from others but also for the tremendous amount of energy it takes to try to be in two heads at once! Think about it for a moment. When you hurry someone along, interrupt someone, or finish his or her sentence, you have to keep track not only of your own thoughts but of those of the person you are interrupting as well. This tendency (which, by the way, is extremely common in busy people), encourages both parties to speed up their speech and their thinking. This, in turn, makes both people nervous, irritable, and annoyed. It's downright exhausting. It's also the cause of many arguments, because if there's one thing almost everyone resents, it's someone who doesn't listen to what they are saying. And how can you really listen to what someone is saying when you are speaking for that person?

Once you begin noticing yourself interrupting others, you'll see this insidious tendency is nothing more than an innocent habit that has become invisible to you. This is good news because it means that all you really have to do is to begin catching yourself when you forget. Remind yourself (before a conversation begins, if possible) to be patient and wait. Tell yourself to allow the other person to finish speaking before you take your turn. You'll notice, right away, how much the interactions with the people in your life will improve as a direct result of this simple act. The people you communicate with will feel much more relaxed around you when they feel heard and listened to. You'll also notice how much more relaxed *you'll* feel when you stop interrupting others. Your heart and pulse rates will slow down, and you'll begin to enjoy your conversations rather than rush through them. This is an easy way to become a more relaxed, loving person.

Be the First One to Act Loving or Reach Out

So many of us hold onto little resentments that may have stemmed from an argument, a misunderstanding, the way we were raised, or some other painful event. Stubbornly, we wait for someone else to reach out to us—believing this is the *only* way we can forgive or rekindle a friendship or family relationship.

An acquaintance of mine, whose health isn't very good, recently told me that she hadn't spoken to her son in almost three years. "Why not?" I asked. She said that she and her son had had a disagreement about his wife and that she wouldn't speak to him again unless he called first. When I suggested that she be the one to reach out, she resisted initially and said, "I can't do that. He's the one who should apologize." She was literally willing to die before reaching out to her only son. After a little gentle encouragement, however, she did decide to be the first one to reach out. To her amazement, her son was grateful for her willingness to call and offered an apology of his own. As is usually the case when someone takes the chance and reaches out, everyone wins.

Whenever we hold on to our anger, we turn "small stuff" into really "big stuff" in our minds. We start to believe that our positions are more important than our happiness. They are not. If you want to be a more peaceful person you must understand that being right is almost never more important than allowing yourself to be happy. The way to be happy is to let go, and reach out. Let other people be right. This doesn't mean that you're wrong. Everything will be fine. You'll experience the peace of letting go, as well as the joy of letting others be right. You'll also notice that, as you reach out and let others be "right," they will become less defensive and more loving toward you. They might even reach back. But, if for some reason they don't, that's okay too. You'll have the inner satisfaction of knowing that you have done your part to create a more loving world, and certainly you'll be more peaceful yourself.

Become Aware of Your Moods and Don't Allow Yourself to Be Fooled by the Low Ones

Your own moods can be extremely deceptive. They can, and probably do, trick you into believing your life is far worse than it really is. When you're in a good mood, life looks great. You have perspective, common sense, and wisdom. In good moods, things don't feel so hard, problems seem less formidable and easier to solve. When you're in a good mood, relationships seem to flow and communication is easy. If you are criticized, you take it in stride.

On the contrary, when you're in a bad mood,

life looks unbearably serious and difficult. You have very little perspective. You take things personally and often misinterpret those around you, as you impute malignant motives into their actions.

Here's the catch: People don't realize their moods are always on the run. They think instead that their lives have suddenly become worse in the past day, or even the last hour. So, someone who is in a good mood in the morning might love his wife, his job, and his car. He is probably optimistic about his future and feels grateful about his past. But by late afternoon, if his mood is bad, he claims he hates his job, thinks of his wife as a nuisance, thinks his car is a junker, and believes he's going nowhere in his career. If you ask him about his childhood while he's in a low mood, he'll probably tell you it was extremely difficult. He will probably blame his parents for his current plight.

Such quick and drastic contrasts may seem absurd, even funny—but we're all like that. In low moods we lose our perspective and everything seems urgent. We completely forget that when we are in a good mood, everything seems so much better. We experience the *identical* circumstances—who we are married to, where we work, the car we drive, our potential, our childhood—entirely different, depending on our mood! When we are low, rather than blaming our mood as would be appropriate, we instead tend to feel that our whole life is wrong. It's almost as if we actually believe our lives have fallen apart in the past hour or two.

The truth is, life is almost *never* as bad as it seems when you're in a low mood. Rather than staying stuck in a bad temper, convinced you are seeing life realistically, you can learn to question your judgment. Remind yourself, "Of course I'm

9

feeling defensive [or angry, frustrated, stressed, depressed]; I'm in a bad mood. I always feel negative when I'm low." When you're in an ill mood, learn to pass it off as simply that: an unavoidable human condition that *will* pass with time, if you leave it alone. A low mood is not the time to analyze your life. To do so is emotional suicide. If you have a legitimate problem, it will still be there when your state of mind improves. The trick is to be grateful for our good moods and graceful in our low moods—not taking them too seriously. The next time you feel low, for whatever reason, remind yourself, "This too shall pass." It will.

4.

Look Beyond Behavior

Have you ever heard yourself, or someone else, say: "Don't mind John, he didn't know what he was doing"? If so, you have been exposed to the wisdom of "looking beyond behavior." If you have children, you know very well the importance of this simple act of forgiveness. If we all based our love on our children's behavior, it would often be difficult to love them at all. If love were based purely on behavior, then perhaps none of us would ever have been loved as a teenager!

Wouldn't it be nice if we could try to extend this same loving-kindness toward everyone we meet? Wouldn't we live in a more loving world if, when someone acted in a way that we didn't approve of, we could see their actions in a similar light as our teenagers' offbeat behavior?

This doesn't mean that we walk around with our heads in the sand, pretending that everything is always wonderful, allow others to "walk all over us," or that we excuse or approve of negative behavior. Instead, it simply means having the perspective to give others the benefit of the doubt. Know that when the postal clerk is moving slowly, he is probably having a bad day, or perhaps all of his days are bad. When your spouse or close friend snaps at you, try to understand that, beneath this isolated act, your loved one really wants to love you, and to feel loved by you. Looking beyond behavior is easier than you might think. Try it today, and you'll see and feel some nice results.

5

Choose Being Kind over Being Right

You are given many opportunities to choose between being kind and being right. You have chances to point out to someone their mistakes, things they could or should have done differently, ways they can improve. You have chances to "correct" people, privately as well as in front of others. What all these opportunities amount to are chances to make someone else feel bad, and yourself feel bad in the process.

Without getting too psychoanalytical about it, the reason we are tempted to put others down, correct them, or show them how we're right and

13

they're wrong is that our ego mistakenly believes that if we point out how someone else is wrong, we must be right, and therefore we will feel better.

In actuality, however, if you pay attention to the way you feel after you put someone down, you'll notice that you feel worse than before the put-down. Your heart, the compassionate part of you, knows that it's impossible to feel better at the expense of someone else.

Luckily, the opposite is true—when your goal is to build people up, to make them feel better, to share in their joy, you too reap the rewards of their positive feelings. The next time you have the chance to correct someone, even if their facts are a little off, resist the temptation. Instead, ask yourself, "What do I really want out of this interaction?" Chances are, what you want is a peaceful interaction where all parties leave feeling good.

Each time you resist "being right," and instead choose kindness, you'll notice a peaceful feeling within.

Recently my wife and I were discussing a business idea that had turned out really well. I was talking about "my" idea, clearly taking credit for the success! Kris, in her usual loving manner, allowed me to have the glory. Later that day, I remembered the idea was actually her idea, not mine. Whoops! When I called her to apologize, it was obvious to me that she cared more for my joy than she did her own need to take credit. She said she enjoys seeing me happy and it doesn't matter whose idea it was. (Do you see why she's so easy to love?)

Don't confuse this strategy with being a wimp, or not standing up for what you believe in. I'm not suggesting that it's not okay for you to be right— only that if you insist on being right, there is often a price to pay—your inner peace. In order to be a person filled with equanimity, you must choose kindness over being right, most of the time. The best place to start is with the next person you speak to.

6

When in Doubt about Whose Turn It Is to Take Out the Trash, Go Ahead and Take It Out

If we're not careful, it's easy to become resentful about all the responsibilities of daily living. Once, in a very low mood, I figured out that on an average day, I do over 1,000 different things. Of course, when I'm in a better mood, that number is significantly lower.

As I think about it, it's astounding to me how easy it is for me to remember all the chores that I do, as well as the other responsibilities that I take care of. But, at the same time, it's easy for me to forget all the things my wife does on a daily basis. How convenient!

It's really difficult to become a contented person if you're keeping score of all you do. Keeping track only discourages you by cluttering your mind with who's doing what, who's doing more, and so forth. If you want to know the truth about it, this is the epitome of "small stuff." It will bring you far more joy to know that you have done your part and someone else in your family has one less thing to do, than it will to worry and fret over whose turn it is to take out the trash.

The strongest argument against this strategy is the concern that you'll be taken advantage of. This mistake is similar to believing it's important that you're right. Most of the time, it's *not* important that you're right, and neither is it important if you take out the trash a few more times than your spouse or housemate. Making things like garbage less relevant in your life will undoubtedly free up more time and energy for truly important things.

7

Develop Your Own Helping Rituals

If you want your life to stand for peace and kindness, it's helpful to do kind, peaceful things. One of my favorite ways to do this is by developing my own helping rituals. These little acts of kindness are opportunities to be of service and reminders of how good it feels to be kind and helpful.

We live in a rural area of the San Francisco Bay Area. Most of what we see is beauty and nature. One of the exceptions to the beauty is the litter that some people throw out of their windows as they are driving on rural roads. One of the few drawbacks to living out in the boondocks is that public services, such as litter collection, are less available than they are closer to the city.

A helping ritual that I practice regularly with my two children is picking up litter in our surrounding area. We've become so accustomed to doing this that my daughters will often say to me in animated voices, "There's some litter, Daddy, stop the car!" And if we have time, we will often pull over and pick it up. It may seem strange, but we actually enjoy it. We pick up litter in parks, on sidewalks, practically anywhere. Once I even saw a complete stranger picking up litter close to where we live. He smiled at me and said, "I saw you doing it, and it seemed like a good idea."

Picking up litter is only one of an endless supply of possible helping rituals. You might like holding a door open for people, visiting lonely elderly people in nursing homes, or shoveling snow off someone else's driveway. Think of something that seems effortless yet helpful. It's fun, personally rewarding, and sets a good example. Everyone wins.

8.

Resist the Urge to Criticize

When we judge or criticize another person, it says nothing about that person; it merely says something about our own need to be critical.

If you attend a gathering and listen to all of the criticism that is typically levied against others, and then go home and consider how much good all that criticism actually does to make the world a better place, you'll probably come up with the same answer that I do: Zero! It does no good. But that's not all. Being critical not only solves nothing; it contributes to the anger and distrust in our world. After all, none of us likes to be criticized. Our reaction to criticism is usually to become defensive and/or withdrawn. A person who feels attacked is likely to do one of two things: He will either retreat in fear or shame, or he will attack or lash out in anger. How many times have you criticized someone and had them respond by saying, "Thank you so much for pointing out my flaws. I really appreciate it"?

Criticism, like swearing, is actually nothing more than a bad habit. It's something we get used to doing; we're familiar with how it feels. It keeps us busy and gives us something to talk about.

If, however, you take a moment to observe how you actually feel immediately after you criticize someone, you'll notice that you will feel a little deflated and ashamed, almost like *you're* the one who has been attacked. The reason this is true is that when we criticize, it's a statement to the world and to ourselves, "I have a need to be critical." This isn't something we are usually proud to admit.

The solution is to catch yourself in the act of being critical. Notice how often you do it and how bad it makes you feel. What I like to do is turn it into a game. I still catch myself being critical, but as my need to criticize arises, I try to remember to say to myself, "There I go again." Hopefully, more often than not, I can turn my criticism into tolerance and respect.

9

Just for Fun, Agree with Criticism Directed Toward You (Then Watch It Go Away)

So often we are immobilized by the slightest criticism. We treat it like an emergency, and defend ourselves as if we were in a battle. In truth, however, criticism is nothing more than observation by another person about us, our actions, or the way we think about something that doesn't match the vision we have of ourselves. Big deal!

When we react to criticism with a knee-jerk, defensive response, it hurts. We feel attacked, and we have a need to defend or to offer a counter-criticism. We fill our minds with angry or hurtful thoughts directed at ourselves or at the person who is being critical. All of this reaction takes an enormous amount of mental energy.

An incredibly useful exercise is to agree with criticism directed toward you. I'm not talking about turning into a doormat or ruining your self-esteem by believing all negativity that comes in your direction. I'm only suggesting that there are many times when simply agreeing with criticism defuses the situation, satisfies a person's need to express a point of view, offers you a chance to learn something about yourself by seeing a grain of truth in another position, and, perhaps most important, provides you an opportunity to stay calm.

One of the first times I consciously agreed with criticism directed toward me was many years ago when my wife said to me, "Sometimes you talk too much." I remember feeling momentarily hurt before deciding to agree. I responded by saying, "You're right, I do talk too much sometimes." I discovered something that changed in my life. In agreeing with her, I was able to see that she had a good point. I often do talk too much! What's more, my non-defensive reaction helped her to relax. A few minutes later she said, "You know, you're sure easy to talk to." I doubt she would have said that had I become angry at her observation. I've since learned that reacting to criticism never makes the criticism go away. In fact, negative reactions to criticism often convince the person doing the criticizing that they are accurate in their assessment of you.

Give this strategy a try. I think you'll discover that agreeing with an occasional criticism has more value than it costs.

10

Relax

What does it mean to relax? Despite hearing this term thousands of times during the course of our lives, very few people have deeply considered what it's really about.

When you ask people (which I've done many times) what it means to relax, most will answer in a way that suggests that relaxing is something you plan to do later—you do it on vacation, in a hammock, when you retire, or when you get everything done. This implies, of course, that most other times (the other 95 percent of your life) should be spent nervous, agitated, rushed, and frenzied. Very few actually come out and say so, but this is the obvious implication. Could this explain why so many of us operate as if life were one great big emergency? Most of us postpone relaxation until our "in basket" is empty. Of course, it never is.

It's useful to think of relaxation as a quality of heart that you can access on a regular basis rather than something reserved for some later time. You can relax now. It's helpful to remember that relaxed people can still be superachievers and, in fact, that relaxation and creativity go hand in hand. When I'm feeling uptight, for example, I don't even try to write. But when I'm relaxed, my writing flows quickly and easily.

Being more relaxed involves training yourself to respond differently to the dramas of life—turning your melodrama into a mellow-drama. It comes, in part, from reminding yourself over and over again (with loving-kindness and patience) that you have a choice in how you respond to life. You can learn to relate to your thinking as well as your circumstances in new ways. With practice, making these choices will translate into a more relaxed self.

11

Think of What You Have Instead of What You Want

In over a dozen years as a stress consultant, one of the most pervasive and destructive mental tendencies I've seen is that of focusing on what we *want* instead of what we *have*. It doesn't seem to make any difference how much we have; we just keep expanding our list of desires, which guarantees we will remain dissatisfied. The mind-set that says, "I'll be happy when this desire is fulfilled" is the same mind-set that will repeat itself once that desire is met.

A friend of ours closed escrow on his new home on a Sunday. The very next time we saw him he was talking about his next house that was going to be even bigger! He isn't alone. Most of us do the very same thing. We want this or that. If we don't get what we want we keep thinking about all that we don't have—and we remain dissatisfied. If we do get what we want, we simply re-create the same thinking in our new circumstances. So, despite getting what we want, we still remain unhappy. Happiness can't be found when we are yearning for new desires.

Luckily, there is a way to be happy. It involves changing the emphasis of our thinking from what we want to what we have. Rather than wishing your spouse was different, try thinking about her wonderful qualities. Instead of complaining about your salary, be grateful you have a job. Rather than wishing you were able to take a vacation to Hawaii, think of how much fun you have had close to home. The list of possibilities is endless! Each time you notice yourself falling into the "I wish life were different" trap, back off and start over. Take a breath and remember all you have to be grateful for. When you focus on the good qualities of your spouse, she'll be more loving. If you are grateful for your job rather than complaining about it, you'll do a better job, be more productive, and probably end up getting a raise anyway. If you focus on ways to enjoy yourself around home rather than waiting to enjoy yourself in Hawaii, you'll end up having more fun. If you ever do get to Hawaii, you'll be in the habit of enjoying yourself. And, if by some chance you don't, you'll have a great life anyway.

Make a note to yourself to start thinking more about what you have than what you want. If you do, your life will start appearing much better than before. For perhaps the first time in your life, you'll know what it means to feel satisfied.

Be Willing to Learn from Friends and Family

One of the saddest observations I've made centers around how reluctant many of us are to learn from the people closest to us—our parents, spouses, children, and friends. Rather than being open to learning, we close ourselves off out of embarrassment, fear, stubbornness, or pride. It's almost as if we say to ourselves, "I have already learned all that I can [or want to learn] from this person; there is nothing else I can [or need to] learn."

It's sad, because often the people closest to us know us the best. They are sometimes able to see ways in which we are acting in a self-defeating manner and can offer very simple solutions. If we are too proud or stubborn to learn, we lose out on some wonderful, simple ways to improve our lives.

I have tried to remain open to the suggestions of my friends and family. In fact, I have gone so far as to ask certain members of my family and a few of my friends, "What are some of my blind spots?" Not only does this make the person you are asking feel wanted and special, but you end up getting some terrific advice. It's such a simple shortcut for growth, yet almost no one uses it. All it takes is a little courage and humility, and the ability to let go of your ego. This is especially true if you are in the habit of ignoring suggestions, taking them as criticism, or tuning out certain members of your family. Imagine how shocked they will be when you ask them, sincerely, for their advice.

Pick something that you feel the person whom you are asking is qualified to answer. For example, I often ask my father for advice on business. Even if he happens to give me a bit of a lecture, it's well worth it. The advice he gives usually prevents me from having to learn something the hard way.

Give Up on the Idea that "More Is Better"

We live in the most affluent culture the world has ever seen. Estimates are that although we have only 6 percent of the world's population in America, we use almost half of the natural resources. It seems to me that if more were actually better, we would live in the happiest, most satisfied culture of all time. But we don't. Not even close. In fact, we live in one of the most dissatisfied cultures on record.

It's not that having a lot of things is bad, wrong, or harmful in and of itself, only that the desire to have more and more and more is insatiable. As long as you think more is better, you'll never be satisfied.

As soon as we get something, or achieve something, most of us simply go on to the next thing—immediately. This squelches our appreciation for life and for our many blessings. I know a man, for example, who bought a beautiful home in a nice area. He was happy until the day after he moved in. Then the thrill was gone. Immediately, he wished he'd bought a bigger, nicer home. His "more is better" thinking wouldn't allow him to enjoy his new home, even for a day. Sadly, he is not unique. To varying degrees, we are all like that. It's gotten to the point that when the Dalai Lama won the Nobel Prize for Peace in 1989, one of the first questions he received from a reporter was "What's next?" It seems that whatever we do—buy a home or a car, eat a meal, find a partner, purchase some clothes, even win a prestigious honor—it's never enough.

The trick in overcoming this insidious tendency is to convince yourself that more isn't better and that the problem doesn't lie in what you don't have, but in the longing for more. Learning to be satisfied doesn't mean you can't, don't, or shouldn't ever want more than you have, only that your happiness isn't contingent on it. You can learn to be happy with what you have by becoming more present-moment-oriented, by not focusing so much on what you want. As thoughts of what would make your life better enter you mind, gently remind yourself that, even if you got what you want, you wouldn't be one bit more satisfied, because the same mind-set that wants more now would want more then.

Develop a new appreciation for the blessings you already enjoy. See your life freshly, as if for the first time. As you develop this new awareness, you'll find that as new possessions or accomplishments enter your life, your level of appreciation will be heightened.

An excellent measure of happiness is the differential between what you have and what you want. You can spend your lifetime wanting more, always chasing happiness—or you can simply decide to consciously want less. The latter strategy is infinitely easier and more fulfilling.

14

Keep in Mind that a Happy Spouse Is a Helping Spouse

This is such an obvious concept that I'm almost embarrassed to write about it. Yet, I've found that very few marriages take advantage of the truly remarkable ramifications of this strategy. The idea, of course, is that when your spouse is happy and feels appreciated, he or she will want to be of help to you! On the other hand, when your spouse feels unhappy and/or taken for granted, the last thing in the world he or she will feel like doing is making *your* life easier!

Let me make it perfectly clear that I'm not suggesting that it's your responsibility to make your spouse happy. It's ultimately up to each person to make that happen for himself or herself. We do, however, play a significant role in whether or not our spouses feel appreciated. Think about your own situation for a moment. How often do you *genuinely* thank your spouse for all of the hard work he or she does on your behalf? I've met hundreds of people who admit to virtually never thanking their spouses in this way, and almost no one who does so on a regular basis.

Your spouse is your partner. Ideally, you'd treat your partner as you would your best friend. If your best friend, for example, said to you, "I would love to get away by myself for a few days," what would you say? In most cases, you'd probably come back with something like, "That sounds great. You deserve it. You should do it." But if your *spouse* said exactly the same thing, would your reaction be the same? Or would you think about how his or her request would affect you? Would you feel put out, defensive, or resentful? Is a good friend more concerned with himself or herself, or with the happiness of the other person? Do you think it's a coincidence that your good friends love to help you whenever possible?

Obviously, you can't always treat your spouse in exactly the same way you would your other good friends. After all, running a marriage and/or household as well as a joint budget carries with it a great deal of responsibility. However, the dynamic can be similar. For example, if a good friend came over and cleaned your house and then took the time to make your dinner, what would you say? How would you react? If your spouse does the very same thing, doesn't he or she deserve the same recognition and gratitude? Most certainly. Whether our jobs involve staying at home, working out of the house, or some combination of the two, we all love and deserve to be appreciated. And when we don't feel taken for granted, our natural instinct is to be of help.

Almost nothing is more predictable than the way people respond when they feel appreciated and valued. Both my wife and I genuinely appreciate each other and try to remember never to take each other for granted. I love it when Kris tells me how much she appreciates all my hard work, and she continues to let me know, even after more than thirteen years of marriage. I also try to remember to acknowledge and express my gratitude daily for her hard work and for her enormous contribution to our family. The result is that we both love to do things for each other—not just out of obligation but because we know that we are appreciated.

You may be doing the same thing already. If so, keep it up. But if not, it's never too late to start. Ask yourself, What could I do to express my gratitude toward my spouse even more than I already do? Usually, the answer is very simple. Make an ongoing effort to say "Thank you," and do so genuinely. Keep in mind not so much what you are doing for the relationship, but what your spouse is doing. Express your gratitude and appreciation. I bet you'll notice what all happy couples do—that the happier and more appreciated your spouse feels, the more often he or she will reach out to help you.

15

Listen to Her (and Him Too)

If I had to pick a single suggestion that was designed to help virtually all relationship and family problems, it would be to become a better listener. And although a vast majority of us need a great deal of work in this area, I'd have to say it's us *men* who need it the most!

Of the hundreds of women I've known over my lifetime, and the thousands I've spoken to through my work, a vast majority complain that a spouse, boyfriend, significant other, or father is a poor listener. And most say that the slightest improvement in the quality of listening would be extremely well received and would undoubtedly make the relationship, regardless of the nature of the relationship, even better. Listening is almost like a "magic pill" that is virtually guaranteed to produce results.

It's interesting to speak to couples who claim they have a loving relationship. In most cases, if you ask them the secret of their success, they will point to the other person's ability to listen as one of the most significant factors that contributes to the quality of their relationship. This is also true of positive father/ daughter, as well as boyfriend/girlfriend, relationships.

Why, then, if the payback is so powerful and certain, do so few of us become good listeners? There are a few reasons that stick out in my mind. First, as far as men are concerned, many of us feel that listening is a nonproactive solution. In other words, when we're listening instead of jumping in, we don't feel as though we're doing anything. We feel we're being too passive. It's hard for us to accept the fact that the listening itself is the solution.

The way to overcome this particular hurdle is to begin to understand how much being listened to is valued by the people we love. When someone genuinely listens to us, it feels as though we are heard and loved. It nourishes our spirits and makes us feel understood. On the other hand, when we don't feel listened to, our hearts sink. We feel as though something is missing; we feel incomplete and dissatisfied.

The other major reason so few of us become good listeners is that we don't realize how bad we really are! But, other than someone telling us about it or pointing it out to us in some way, how could we know? Our poor listening skills become an invisible habit that we don't even realize we have.

And because we have so much company, our listening skills probably seem more than adequate—so we don't give it much thought.

Determining how effective you are as a listener takes a great deal of honesty and humility. You have to be willing to quiet down and listen to yourself as you jump in and interrupt someone. Or you have to be a little more patient and observe yourself as you walk away, or begin thinking of something else, before the person you are speaking to has finished.

This is about as close as you're going to get to a virtually guaranteed result. You may be amazed at how quickly old problems and issues correct themselves and how much closer you will feel to the ones you love if you simply quiet down and become a better listener. Becoming a better listener is an art form, yet it's not at all complicated.

Mostly, all it requires is your intention to become a better listener, followed by a little practice. I'm sure you effort will be well worth it!

16.

Keep Your Promises

In my opinion, no book on improving family life would be complete without at least a few words on keeping your promises. This is an extremely powerful, long-term strategy to keep you permanently bonded with those you love. You can do a lot of things wrong, but if you keep your promises, you'll be richly rewarded in terms of the quality of your relationship and the integrity that others will perceive that you will have. On the other hand, if you fail to keep your promises, those around you—even your own family—will take your words less seriously, or even worse, learn to distrust you altogether.

Obviously, no one is perfect, and there will be times when you fail to keep a promise for a variety of reasons—you'll forget, or something "pressing" will come up. In most cases, this isn't a problem because keeping your promises isn't an all-or-nothing proposition but a lifetime process. In other words, your goal isn't to be perfect but to strive to keep as many as your promises as possible.

Not too long ago, I had promised to attend my daughter's soccer game, but a few weeks later was given the opportunity to appear on a major national talk show to discuss *Don't Sweat the Small Stuff*. All things considered, I needed to go. My daughter was truly disappointed. I felt like a successful parent, however, when she gave me a hug through her tears and said, "It's all right, Daddy. This is the very first game you've missed this year." My record wasn't perfect, as it rarely is, but it was pretty darn good. My daughter knew that when I said "I really wish I could be there," my words weren't hollow. She knew that my promises are important to me and I really try hard to keep them. Like most people, she doesn't expect perfection, only an honest attempt to live with integrity, to do the best I can.

It's also important to keep your more subtle or implied promises. If, for example, you tell your mother, "I'll give you a call tomorrow," make every attempt to do so. So often we will say things—make subtle promises—because it makes the moment a little easier, or makes someone feel special for the time being, but we fail to deliver, thus more than erasing the positive effect of our good intentions. We'll say things like, "I'll swing by later this afternoon," or "I'll be there no later than six o'clock." But, time and time again, we don't actually come through. We rationalize our promises by saying things like, "I tried, but I'm really busy," but that is of little consolation to someone who is on the receiving end. To most people, a broken promise is more evidence that promises don't mean very much.

I have found that it's much better not to make a promise, even if you want to, unless you're relatively certain you'll be able to keep it. If you're not certain you're going to actually do something for someone, don't say you're going to. Make it a surprise instead. Or if you're not sure you're going to call, don't say you *are* going to call, and so forth.

By keeping our promises we do our little part in helping our loved ones keep their cynicism to a minimum. We teach them that some people can be trusted and are trustworthy. You may be pleasantly surprised at how much people will appreciate you when you do what you say you are going to do, when you keep your promises. Your life at home and around your family will be greatly enhanced.

17

Never Miss a Chance to Say
"I Love You"

In my lifetime I've heard many people complain that their parents (or their spouses) either never or seldom said (or say) "I love you." On the other end of the spectrum, I've never heard a single person complain that his or her parents, or anyone else, said these words too often.

I can't imagine anything easier than saying the words "I love you." However, for whatever reasons, many people don't do so. Perhaps we don't believe that our loved ones need to hear it, that they don't want to, or that they won't believe it. Or perhaps we're too stubborn or shy. Whatever the reason, it's not good enough. There are simply too many important reasons to tell the people in your life that you love them.

Whether you heard these words enough in your life or not is not the issue. At issue here is the fact that saying "I love you" makes people feel good. It reminds them that they are not alone and that you do care. It raises their self-esteem—and it makes *you* feel good too! Undoubtedly, in my family, we do many things wrong. One thing we do right, however, is tell each other how much we love each other. It's simple, painless, and free. It's one of the most powerful sentences in the world. People who know they are loved (because they have been told) are able to offer the world their love in return. They have a quiet confidence and a sense of inner peace.

One of my firmest beliefs is that when you have

what you want (in an emotional sense), your natural inclination is to give back to others. So, by saying "I love you" to a single person, you are, indirectly, helping the world at large. There is perhaps no way to guarantee that someone will feel loved and appreciated. But certainly the way to increase the odds is to tell him or her so, frequently. Genuinely saying the words "I love you" can erase many mistakes in the eyes of your loved ones. I know, for example, that when I've had difficult times with my kids, remembering to tell them that I love them has helped us to forgive one another and move on.

On a more selfish note, saying "I love you" has personal benefits as well. It feels good. Since giving and receiving are two sides of the same coin, saying the words "I love you" more than makes up for not hearing them enough in your lifetime. It's absolutely true that giving is its own reward. And saying these loving words is one of the most basic and simple forms of giving.

There are so many opportune times to express your love in this manner—when you enter the house, right before you leave, before bed, and first thing in the morning. In our family, we have developed the habit of saying "I love you" before hanging up the telephone when we're talking to one another, as well as before we begin eating a family meal. Your opportunities are unlimited. This will be one of the easiest things you'll ever do—and, when all is said and done, one of the most important.

18

Fill Your Home with Evidence of Love

There are so many distractions in life and reminders of the problems we all must deal with that it's critical to counter this bombardment of negativity with evidence of love. Kris and I have found that it's relatively simple (and can be very inexpensive) to fill your home with evidence of love and happiness. And when you do, you are constantly reminded of the positive aspects of life.

Evidence of love can be anything beautiful, special to your heart, artistic, airy, or light—anything that reminds you of love, kindness, gentleness, and compassion. It can be the artwork of children, fresh-cut flowers, beautiful poetry or philosophy hanging on your wall, spiritual and loving books on your coffee table, or photographs of your loved ones. An acquaintance of mine writes positive, loving affirmations in calligraphy and tapes them to her refrigerator. Others save heartfelt letters and pin them on a bulletin board.

Comedian Steve Martin used to do a hilarious skit in which he played the banjo and sang about how difficult it is to be depressed while doing so. The banjo is so upbeat and happy sounding that, while you're playing it, it makes negativity and unhappiness seem a little silly. In a way, filling your home with evidence of love has a similar flavor to it. It's not impossible, but it's certainly more difficult, to get too worked up, stressed out, or depressed when there are signs of love and beauty everywhere you look.

In our home, we have photographs of friends, family, and spiritual people on many different walls. We regularly update, move around, and change the photos to keep them current and interesting. We also have great books that emphasize love visible in virtually every room, as well as beautiful artwork made for us by the kids. I'm certain that if I didn't have kids I'd ask friends or neighbors if I could have a few of their extras. In many families there is plenty to go around, and when you ask children if they will draw you a picture, many are honored to do so. The artwork of children is so uplifting, and is such a reminder of love, that I can't imagine not having plenty of it in my home. Our daughters also love to go outside and pick flowers from our yard and bring them into the house to put into water.

There is no specific way to go about implementing this strategy. It's simply a mind-set. Once you see the logic behind it and feel the positive effects, I'm sure you'll be hooked. There is simply no downside to this idea. Starting today, begin filling your home with even more evidence of love. Every time you walk in the door, you'll be glad you did.

19

Start the Day with Love, Live the Day with Love, End the Day with Love

If any of us could master this strategy to its fullest, we would be among the great role models of humanity, right up there with the likes of Mother Teresa. Yet, as difficult as this strategy would be to master, it's worth every bit of effort you put into it.

Actually, the wisdom of this strategy is quite simple. The idea is to remind yourself frequently, throughout the day, of the importance of living your life with *love* as your absolute top priority. Something magical happens to your life when nothing is seen as more important as love. "Small stuff" is kept in its proper perspective and consciousness opens to the beauty and joy of life. Our day-to-day living begins to take on an extraordinary quality and we begin to experience what's truly most important in life.

"Start the day with love" means that when you wake up in the morning, you open your heart and remind yourself of your intent to be loving in every aspect of your life. "Live the day with love" means that your choices and actions stem from your decision to be loving, patient, kind, and gentle. It means you keep things in perspective and try *not* to take things personally or blow things out of proportion. It means you make allowances for the imperfections of others and of yourself, and that you make an effort to keep your criticisms and judgments from rising to the surface. Living the day with love suggests that, whenever possible, you will make an effort to be generous and complimentary, as well as humble and sincere. "End the day with love" means that you take a moment at the close of your day to reflect and be grateful. Perhaps you say a prayer or do a quiet meditation. You might look back on your day and review how closely your *goal* of living with love matched up with your actions and choices. You do this not to keep score, or to be hard on yourself, but simply to experience the peace associated with loving intent and to see areas where you might act even more loving tomorrow.

20

Never, Ever, Take Your Spouse (or Significant Other) for Granted

I could write an entire book on this subject. But, since I have only a few paragraphs to explain, I'll get right to the heart of the matter.

If you take your spouse for granted, it is absolutely 100 percent guaranteed to adversely affect your relationship. I've never, ever, met a single person who likes to be taken for granted—and very few who will put up with it, over the long run.

Clearly, one of the most disrespectful and destructive things we can possibly do to our spouses (or anyone) is to take them for granted. To do so is sort of like saying, "It's your job to make my life easier and my job to expect it." Ouch!

There are so many ways we take our partners for granted. Here are just a few: We take *our* roles more seriously than theirs. We think our contributions are significant and that our partners are "the lucky ones." Many of us forget to say please and thank you—some of us never do. We fail to reflect on how lucky we are or how sad and difficult it would be to live without our spouses. Sometimes we get very demanding of our spouses or treat them much differently than we would a friend. Other times, we speak "for them" or disrespectfully about them in front of others. Some of us think we know what our spouses are thinking, so we make decisions for them. Then there is the common mistake of coming to expect certain things—a clean home or a hot meal. Or money to pay the bills, or a nice clean-cut lawn. They are, after all, our spouses. They should do these things. Finally, very few of us really listen to our spouses or share in their excitement—unless, of course, it matches something we are interested in. I could go on and on, but you get the point.

Is it any wonder that close to 50 percent of marriages end in divorce and that many of the rest are painful, boring, and/or less than satisfying? Hardly! It's so obvious, but for some reason we keep making the same mistake—we take our partners for granted.

The reverse is also true—almost nothing makes people feel better than feeling as though they are appreciated and valued. Think about how wonderful it felt when you first met your spouse or significant other. It was absolutely wonderful. And a major contributing factor to this feeling of love you shared was that you truly appreciated each other. You said things like "It's so nice to hear from you" and "Thank you for calling." You expressed your appreciation for everything from a simple compliment to the tiniest gift, card, or gesture of kindness. Each chance you had, you expressed your gratitude, and you never took your new love for granted.

Many people believe it's inevitable that couples will lose their sense of appreciation for one another. Not so! Appreciation is something you have 100 percent of control over. If you choose to be grateful and to express your appreciation, you will do so. And the more you do so, the more you'll be in the healthy habit of noticing things to be grateful for—it's a self-fulfilling prophesy.

My wife, Kris, is one of the most appreciative people I've ever known. She's constantly telling me how much she loves me or how lucky she is to be married to me. I try to remember to do the same because that's exactly how I feel. And you know what? Every time she expresses her appreciation toward me, I feel that much more love toward her. And she assures me the same is true for her. But we don't do this as a way of getting love, but simply because we both tend to focus on how lucky we are to have one another as a friend and partner.

For example, I'll be away at a speaking engagement and Kris will leave me a sweet message telling me how grateful she is that I'm willing to work so hard for our family. About the same time, I'll leave a message with her, letting her know how grateful I am that she's willing and able to be home with our children, giving them the love they need and deserve, while I'm away. We both honestly feel that the other is making at least an equal sacrifice and that, regardless, we're on the same team. Then, when she's away and I'm home, it seems we reverse compliments. She's grateful that I'm willing and able to be at home and I'm equally grateful that she's away making yet another contribution to our family.

Kris and I have been together for more than fifteen years, and we love each other more today than we did all those years ago. I'm absolutely certain that our decision *not* to take each other for granted is one of the major reasons why this is true. I'll bet you'll be shocked at how powerful this strategy can be if you give it a try. For the time being, forget what you are getting back and focus only on what you are giving. I believe that if you make the decision to stop taking your partner for granted, in time your spouse will begin to do the same thing. It feels good to be grateful. Try it, you'll love it!

21

Appreciate Your In-laws

Admittedly, this has been an easy one for me because my in-laws, Pat and Ted, are extraordinary people. And I must say that my wife is equally lucky because my parents are also quite special. However, for most people, in-laws present quite a personal challenge, to say the least. And even if you like your in-laws, you do have to make certain sacrifices simply because of the nature of marriage. You will, for example, have to make trade-offs as to where you spend holidays. You will also have to deal with the most unavoidable problems of conflicting backgrounds and upbringings—different religious philosophies, differing views on parenting, discipline, spending, saving, the relative importance of spending time with family, and so forth. Yet, despite probable differences among you, I believe that most in-law relationships have the potential to be loving and filled with mutual respect.

The trick to making the most of your relationship with your in-laws is to stay focused on gratitude. While there almost certainly will be differences you will have to deal with, gratitude will enable you to appreciate, rather than struggle against, those differences.

It's easy to forget, yet if you love your spouse, you owe your in-laws and enormous debt of gratitude! If not for their bringing your spouse into the world, you would be with someone else, or alone. In most instances, it took your in-laws (or one of them) to raise your spouse. So, regardless of what you may think, they played a significant role in your spouse's upbringing.

Before you sarcastically think something like, "That explains why my spouse has certain problems," keep in mind that the opposite is equally true. If you blame your in-laws for any issues your spouse struggles with, it's only fair to give them credit for his or her strengths as well. In addition, if you have children, their genes—their physical makeup—come, in part, from your in-laws. Without their contribution, your children would not be the people they are. If you think your kids are cute, and who doesn't think so, some of that cuteness, whether you want to believe it or not, comes from your in-laws.

Believe me, I'm not a bury-your-head-in-the-sand-and-pretend-everything-is-perfect kind of person. I realize that all in-laws have certain difficult qualities, just as I will to my future son-in-law, someday down the road (way down the road). However, what choice do you have? You can continue to complain about your in-laws, make mean-spirited jokes about how difficult it is to have them, and wish that they were different—or you can begin to focus less on their irritating quirks and characteristics and instead focus on that which you have to be grateful for. I believe the decision is an easy one. Stay focused on gratitude and my guess is that you'll be able to improve your existing relationship in a significant way.

22

Work on Absolute Acceptance
of Those You Love Most

It's sad, but in many cases the people we love unconditionally the *least* are the people we love the *most*. In other words, while we can easily overlook or simply ignore the negativity or idiosyncrasies of complete strangers, it's difficult to do the same with our children or spouses.

This was brought to my attention by a dear friend of mine who noticed my very high expectations of my two daughters. She said to me, "It seems to me that in many areas of your parenting you are quite accepting, but are you aware that, to a large degree, you seem to expect your children to always be enthusiastic and happy?" She went on to ask, "Can you imagine how difficult that expectation would be to live up to?" It was like a whack on the side of my head! Her observation hurt a little, but boy was it right on. It has turned out to be an important insight that has helped me a great deal.

My friend was absolutely right. For the most part, I'm perfectly okay with the fact that most people aren't always happy. I believe I do an excellent job at accepting people exactly as they are. However, I had developed the habit of acting very disappointed in my own children virtually anytime they expressed any emotion other than happiness.

What I learned was that I, like most people, levy my most demanding expectations on those people whom I love the most. Think about some obvious examples: If a neighbor spilled a glass of milk on the floor, you'd probably say, "Oh, don't worry about it, I'll clean it up," but if your child did the exact same thing, would you act the same? Or might you act disappointed, angry, or frustrated? Yet, your child is the one you love with all your heart—not your neighbor. Or you might be very accepting of the "innocent" little quirks of a family friend but feel as if you're going to be driven crazy by your spouse's quirks, even though they are very similar.

I don't want to get overly analytical here about the reasons for this twisted set of values. I believe what's most important is that we recognize our own tendency to have extremely high expectations for our loved ones and that we set out to love more unconditionally. In my case, what was most helpful was to practice remembering that people are different in the ways they express themselves—including my own children. I needed to respect my children and their ways of being in the same ways that I have always tried to respect everyone else. And you know what, it really works! I believe my children have sensed my sincere desire to become less judgmental and more unconditionally loving. And I have felt a similar love coming from each of them. If you make it a top priority to accept those whom you love the most, I think you'll be richly rewarded by the love you'll feel in your family.

23.

Don't Sweat the Little Quirks

In some ways, it's no wonder that the people you live with can drive you crazy with their little quirks. You know, the way someone eats, uses utensils, breathes, flits her hair, jiggles his leg, stacks pennies, or stomps his or her feet, or whatever. After all, chances are you spend more time with these people than anyone else. Therefore, you have far more opportunities to experience and become familiar with the quirks and idiosyncrasies of your family than you do with anyone else. Over time, you come to expect, even anticipate, these quirks, and when they occur they tend to annoy you.

Let's face it. There isn't a person alive who doesn't have his or her share of irritating quirks. I have so many I'd be embarrassed to share them with you. And if you were really honest, I'll bet you'd admit to having a few of your own. But despite these innocent quirks, I'll bet you're a really nice person with many fine qualities. I'd like to think I fall into the same category.

The point is, we're all human. Whether you live alone and only have to deal with your *own* little quirks (or those of any pets you might have), or whether you have a spouse and a bunch of kids and have dozens of quirks to contend with on a regular basis, we're all in this together. To be human is to have quirks. Big deal!

Many people are easily bothered by their own quirks and by those of their family members. They focus on them and wish they would go away. They share their displeasure with their closest friends. But guess what? The chances of those pesky quirks going away are about as good as my chances of winning the Wimbledon tennis championship—zero, none. Okay, maybe once in a great while someone will outgrow an annoying quirk and/or change a pattern or habit. But this is extremely rare and, in most cases, highly unlikely. Think about it. Doesn't the friend in whom you're confiding regarding your spouse's irritating quirks have a few of his or her own? What's more, do you think your friend might, on occasion, discuss *your* little imperfections with his or her other friends?

You really only have two options when it comes to dealing with quirks. You can continue to be critical of, and be bothered by, the little quirks that exist in your household. Or you can choose to see the innocence and humor that is inherent in virtually all quirks. After all, no one wants annoying quirks to be part of his or her personal makeup—we certainly don't set out to create them! They develop unintentionally and continue out of pure habit. In addition, it's important to keep in mind that, if you were to live with someone else, he or she too would quickly exhibit a variety of quirks. And who knows? They might be even more annoying than the ones you are currently forced to deal with.

Why not make the decision to make those little quirks a little less relevant? Doing so is a huge relief. You will no longer have to spend mental energy reminding yourself how irritated you are—therefore feeling the effects of that irritation. And you'll find that when you're more forgiving and accepting of everyone else, it's far easier to be easier on yourself. So, starting today, whatever "small stuff" around the house bugs you, see if you can let it go! You'll be so much happier as a result.

24

Reverse Roles with Your Spouse

It's sad, yet the easiest person to take for granted is probably the person you love most in the world—your spouse. It's so easy to get lost in your own world and set of real-life responsibilities that you begin to believe that your spouse has it much easier than you do, or you forget (or perhaps you don't even realize) how hard your spouse works on your behalf. This tendency can create a great deal of resentment yet is, to a large degree, very preventable. The key to prevention is to put yourself in your spouse's shoes.

I'm going to give an example here *knowing* that

there are millions of exceptions to this stereotype. I'm aware that in today's world many, if not most, families have two income earners and that many, if not most, families share many of the responsibilities at home. I'm also aware that women are often the ones who work while men stay home with the kids. See if you can see through my stereotypical examples, however, to the heart of an important message.

Many of my own male friends have fallen into the trap of taking their spouses for granted. I'm happy to report, however, that some have been helped by taking this strategy to heart. A common example is a man who works and is married to a woman who stays at home (and of course she works hard too). In this typical chauvinistic example, the husband convinces himself that his wife is lucky and often minimizes the importance of her role. He believes that her needs are being met while he's out working all day. He rarely contributes much at home in the way of chores, children, and household responsibilities. He feels put out when asked to do the simplest of things. He's absolutely aware of how hard he works but takes his wife's role completely for granted.

It's shocking (but often very good for a marriage) in cases like this for the husband to take over the home for a week, or even a few days, while his wife visits friends and takes a break. Many men are so frightened by this suggestion that they get the point before they are actually forced to go through the experience. They often realize, when push comes to shove, that they are absolutely incapable of doing the important daily tasks of running a home and raising children. They also realize how exhausting it can be. This is truly hard work! The idea, of course, in switching roles is to regain a sense of gratitude as well as compassion for what one person does for the other.

Of course, this strategy works both ways. It's also very common for a stay-at-home mom to take her husband for granted. She might, for example, complain about the late nights or missed dinners without fully realizing how difficult it can be to earn a living. In most instances, it's unrealistic for a nonworking spouse to actually reverse roles for a week. However, she (or he) could really benefit from trying to imagine what it would be like to actually go out and earn enough money to satisfy the financial needs of her (or his) family. This can be a shocking realization for someone who doesn't actually have a job.

The point of this mental exercise is not to determine whose job is more difficult or important but to recognize the importance and inherent difficulty in both aspects of life. Regardless of your personal situation, and even if you and your spouse both work and both help out at home, it can be enormously helpful to experiment and play around with this strategy. If you do, I think you'll begin to realize and appreciate how much your spouse does for you and how difficult his or her life can be at times. And I can assure you that everyone loves to be appreciated; when people are appreciated, they are more fun to be around.

25

Don't Go to Bed Mad

I learned this bit of wisdom from my parents, and I've appreciated it my entire life. While I was growing up, this family philosophy cut short, or nipped in the bud, many arguments, angry evenings, and negative feelings that would have undoubtedly carried forward to the next day, or perhaps even longer. The idea is that, despite the fact that all families have their share of problems and issues to contend with, nothing is so bad it's worth going to bed mad over. What this strategy ensures is that, regardless of what's happening, who's to blame, or how mad you or someone else in the family happens to be, there is a set cap or limit to your anger, at which time everyone in the family agrees it's time to let go, forgive, apologize, and start over. No exceptions. This limit is bedtime.

When you have an absolute policy that no one goes to bed mad, it helps you remember that love and forgiveness are never far away. It encourages you to bend a little, to be the first to reach out and open the dialogue, offer a genuine hug, and keep your heart open. When you make the decision to never go to bed mad, it helps you see the innocence in your own behavior and in that of your family members. It keeps the channels of communication open. It reminds you that you are a family and that, despite your problems and disagreements, you love, need, and treasure each other. The decision that it's never a good idea to go to bed mad is a built-in reset button that protects your family from stress, hostility, and resentment.

Perhaps it's easier to see the importance of such a policy in its absence. Without a family policy such as this, arguments and anger are open-ended. No one will have created a boundary, a set of rules that protect your family from extended and unnecessary anger. Without a rule to suggest otherwise, family members can hold on to their anger and justify doing so.

Kris and I have tried very hard to implement this strategy in our family. While it's not perfect, and while occasionally one or more of us seems a little frustrated at bedtime, on balance it's been enormously helpful. It ensures that ninety-nine times out of one hundred, we'll wake up the next morning with love in our hearts and with an attitude of "This is a new day." I hope that you'll give this strategy a fair try. It's certainly not always easy, and you probably won't bat 100 percent, but it's well worth the effort. Remember, life is short. Nothing is so important that it's worth ruining your day, nor is anything so significant that it's worth going to bed mad. Have a nice sleep.